Omaha, Nebraska

James and the Sword of the Spirit

Text and Art © 2018 Terrica Joseph. All rights reserved.
All rights reserved. No part of this book may be used or reproduced in any manner whatsoever without permission except in the case of brief quotations embodied in critical articles or reviews.

ISBN 978-1-970016-38-3 (Hardcover Ed)
ISBN 978-1-970016-39-0 (Paperback Ed)
Cataloging-in-Publication date on file with the publisher.

Published by Fruit Springs, LLC
17330 W Center Rd Ste. 110-342
Omaha, NE 68130

Illustrated by: Maryna Kovinka
Design and production: Fruit Springs, LLC

Printed in the United States of America
10 9 8 7 6 5 4 3 2 1

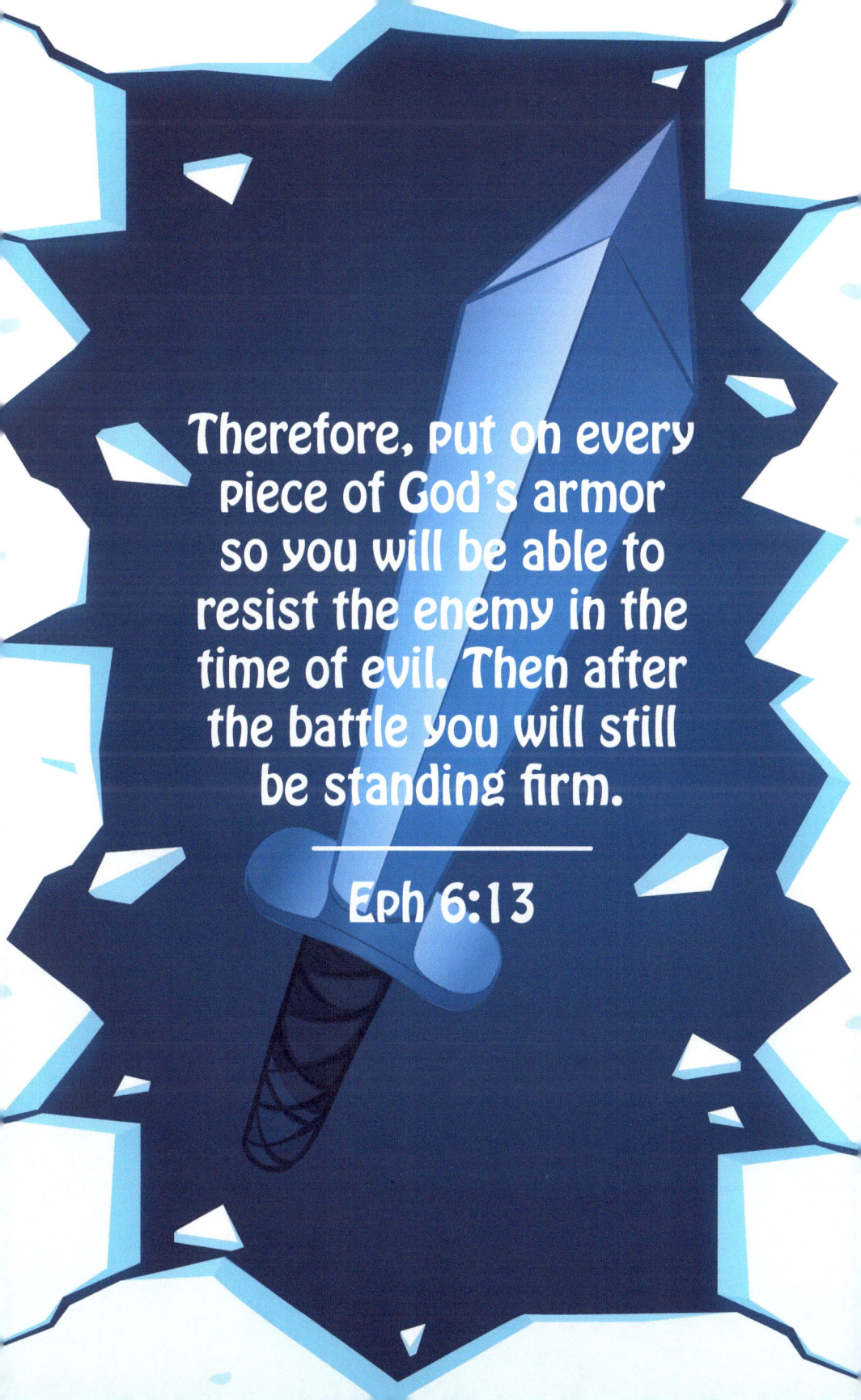

It was a cold morning. James was shoveling the snow off of the sidewalk. He was determined to clear the path for any visitors.

Winters were tough but this year it was bone chilling and he didn't want them to freeze before they reached the door.

James wished for spring to arrive. His toes were frozen and his fingers were numb. It was simply too cold.

Early he discovered that the mailbox was frozen too. James wondered what would freeze next. He was sure if he stayed out any longer he would be frozen like the mailbox, unable to budge.

Mom called James inside for breakfast out of the cold winter air.
"I'm almost done clearing the snow," said James.
"I don't want you to become an icicle," Mom replied.

"It's too late. My eyes are already frozen open. I can't blink anymore," said James.
"If you don't come in soon, your mouth may be frozen shut too," said Mom
"There's no way I would miss eating my pancakes," said James.

James smelled the warm pancakes his mother had prepared.
"I'm ready for breakfast," said James.

"Are you sure about that? Let me take a look at your hands," said Mom.
"I'll be back in a moment," said James.
Being on time was never a problem for James but being prepared was another story.

James ate his breakfast and thought about school.
"What's wrong James?" Mom asked.
"Oh nothing," he replied.

He didn't want to tell her about the trouble at school but he knew she would find out any way.

"There is a new kid at school named Tommy. He's really mean. He stares at me like I'm piece of meat. It's scary," said James.

"Have you tried saying hello?" asked Mom.
"Emma tried but he's too scary."
"Sometimes things that look scary are not bad at all," Mom replied.

James thought about what Mom had said. "We gave him a chance but he growled at us, now I'm stuck with him."
"What do you mean?" asked Mom.

"Ms. Kane wants us to work together. It's not a good idea," said James.
"It's a great idea. Every challenge is an opportunity for you to learn and grow. Just remember the Armor of God and you'll do great."

James thought about the armor of God. He wasn't sure it could help him.
"Do you really think the armor can help me?" James asked.
"Yes, it can. After breakfast, you can use it to take Mrs. Whitaker the dishes I've prepared for her," said Mom.

"What about the dogs? They will eat me," said James.
"You'll be okay. Remember you are strong and courageous and you have the Armor of God," Mom replied.

James hoped the armor would keep him safe from those dogs. He worried as he walked to Mrs. Whitaker's house. They weren't terrible dogs, but they were big and scary. James approached the gate and took a deep breath.

He hoped Mrs. Whitaker's dogs, Peebles and Spike, would be inside but they were both outside to greet him. James hoped the Armor of God was all he would need.

James stood quietly looking at the distance between the gate and the door. He wondered if giving Mrs. Whitaker the warm meal was worth the risk. He wanted to set the food inside of the gate but he knew that wouldn't be right.

Pebbles and Spike would eat the food. They could eat him too. He remembered the conversation he had with his mom and decided he had to be brave.

James walked toward the gate.
"Don't come in. Tell your mother she's not home," Peebles and Spike growled.
"The word of God says not to lie, and I won't," James replied.
"You should be afraid we have sharp teeth."

"God told me to not be afraid and I won't," James replied.
"But you're alone and there's two of us," they growled.
"The Lord is with me wherever I go. I am never alone," said James.

James bravely pushed open the gate. "Are you tired of being nice. Leave and go home," the dogs bark.
"God says we should not grow weary in doing good," James replied.

James was no longer afraid. He was a conqueror.
"You're not brave enough to go to the door," they barked.
"God says to be strong and courageous and I will be," said James.

James faced Peebles and Spike.
"We can protect ourselves but who will protect you," they barked.
"Sit," James said, sternly. The Lord is my protector."

Immediately, Peebles and Spike sat. James knocked on the door and waited for Mrs. Whitaker. He looked back and realized those two dogs weren't so mighty after all. James gave her the food and said goodbye.

James stopped in front of Peebles and Spike. "You are not ferocious dogs. You are not bigger than my God, nor mightier than the Sword," said James.

Peebles and Spike watched as James walked courageously out of the gate. James waved goodbye and went home. He was glad he had the Armor of God.

"Mom, I did it. I did it," James yelled.
"What did you do?" she asked.
"I used the Sword of the Spirit and it worked. It really worked!" said James.

"I knew it would and it always will," Mom replied.
James was ready for school. He knew the Armor would help him there too. He had a mighty Sword that could do amazing things. He would never put it away.

www.ingramcontent.com/pod-product-compliance
Lightning Source LLC
Chambersburg PA
CBHW041809040426
42449CB00001B/27